WHEN **pets** ATTACK!

ALLIGATORS ARE NOT PETS!

Gareth Stevens Publishing

BY MARK HARASYMIW

Please visit our website, www.garethstevens.com. For a free color catalog of all our high-quality books, call toll free 1-800-542-2595 or fax 1-877-542-2596.

Library of Congress Cataloging-in-Publication Data

Harasymiw, Mark
Alligators are not pets / by Mark Harasymiw
pg. cm. — (When pets attack)
Includes index.
ISBN 978-1-4339-9279-7 (pbk)
ISBN 978-1-4339-9280-3 (6-Pack)
ISBN 978-1-4339-9278-0 (library binding)
1. Alligators as pets — Juvenile literature. 2. Wild animals as pets — Juvenile literature. I. Harasymiw, Mark. II. Title.
QL666.C9 H25 2014
597.98—dc23

First Edition

Published in 2014 by
Gareth Stevens Publishing
111 East 14th Street, Suite 349
New York, NY 10003

Designer: Katelyn E. Reynolds
Editor: Therese Shea

Photo credits: Cover, p. 1 Mammut Vision/Shutterstock.com; cover, pp. 1–32 (home sweet home image) © iStockphoto.com/DNY59; cover, pp. 1–32 (background) Hemera/Thinkstock.com; cover, pp. 1–32 (blood splatter), pp. 3–32 (frame) iStockphoto/Thinkstock.com; pp. 5, 7 (both), 19 iStockphoto/Thinkstock.com; p. 8 Hemera/Thinkstock.com; p. 9 vigi veranda/Wikipedia.com; p. 11 Jonathan S. Blair/National Geographic/Getty Images; p. 13 Brian Lasenby/Shutterstock.com; p. 15 Joe Raedle/Getty Images; p. 17 © iStockphoto.com/keewizane; p. 18 Marco Simoni/Robert Harding World Imagery/Getty Images; p. 21 Chel Beeson/Photolibrary/Getty Images; pp. 22–23 mark higgins/Shutterstock.com; p. 25 Otis Imboden/Nationa Geographic/Getty Images; p. 27 Elyse Butler/Aurora/Getty Images; p. 29 Richard Nowitz/National Geographic/Getty Images.

Printed in the United States of America

CPSIA compliance information: Batch #CS13GS: For further information contact Gareth Stevens, New York, New York at 1-800-542-2595.

CONTENTS

Words in the glossary appear in **bold** type the first time they are used in the text.

TOO SCARY TO PET

Most animals that make good pets are smaller than people. Those that aren't smaller, such as horses, eat plants. Adult alligators are bigger than people and like to eat only one thing—MEAT! Alligators are awesome animals to see at the zoo, but they don't make good pets.

A full-grown male alligator may grow more than 13 feet (4 m) long and weigh over 500 pounds (227 kg). Females are about half as heavy and grow to be about 9 feet (2.7 m) long. Smaller doesn't mean less dangerous, though. Mother alligators are fierce when protecting their babies.

growth SPURTS

Depending on **environment** and age, alligators grow at different rates. In warm conditions, a young alligator grows quickly. An alligator in hot Louisiana may grow as much as 12 inches (30 cm) a year. One of the largest alligators ever found in that state was 19 feet 2 inches (5.8 m) long!

Alligators have long lives. They can live about 40 years in the wild, and some in zoos have lived even longer.

WARM-WEATHER CREATURES

Alligators are only found in the southeastern United States and China. They live in freshwater lakes, rivers, ponds, swamps, and marshes. Alligators don't spend much time in salt water like crocodiles do. Crocodiles have special **glands** on their tongue that allow them to force salt out of their bodies. Alligators don't have this ability.

In the wild, American alligators are found all over Florida and Louisiana and along the coasts of Texas, Mississippi, Alabama, Georgia, South Carolina, and North Carolina. Alligators also live in the waterways of Arkansas and even in southeastern Oklahoma.

crocodile OR ALLIGATOR?

Crocodiles and alligators look similar. However, the trained eye can tell them apart. The heads of the reptiles are different. Alligators have a wider **snout** than crocodiles. Also, when an alligator's mouth is closed, their teeth don't show much. The fourth tooth in a crocodile's lower jaw sticks up over its upper lip.

From these photos, you can see some differences between these reptiles' snouts.

Alligators need to be warm. Alligators transported to cold places may die without proper care.

Alligators live in warm places because they're cold-blooded. This means they use outside heat to maintain their body temperature. Alligators commonly warm up by lying in the hot sun or swimming to warmer waters. If they need to cool down, they move to shade or cooler waters.

icy NOSES

When the weather turns cold, some alligators put their noses at the water's surface so they can breathe. Ice may freeze around them! The alligators stay there until the ice melts. Sometimes they get caught below the ice, but alligators have been able to survive up to 8 hours without taking a breath.

Alligators are most active when they're in temperatures between 82°F and 92°F (28°C and 33°C). When the temperature drops below 70°F (21°C), they stop feeding. Below 55°F (13°C), alligators become **dormant**. When winter arrives, alligators dig dens and tunnels to live in until the cold weather passes.

Alligators in the United States

ALLIGATOR COMEBACK

Alligators have long been hunted for their skin and meat. Alligator leather is used for some kinds of clothing. Alligator hunting wasn't overseen until the animals were in danger of becoming **extinct**. In the 1970s and 1980s, strict laws were passed to protect them. The laws were a success. Today, millions of alligators are found in all the areas they lived before they were **endangered**.

Since alligators are no longer in danger of dying out, some states have allowed them to be hunted again. However, American crocodiles are endangered, so alligator hunting is carefully watched over to make sure crocodiles aren't caught by mistake.

alligator farms AND RANCHES

Today, many alligators are raised on farms so there's less need to hunt them. Alligator farms raise alligators from eggs laid there. Alligator ranches are similar to alligator farms. However, ranches gather eggs and babies, or hatchlings, from the wild. Because of its ranches, Louisiana has the largest population of alligators in the world.

Though the Chinese alligator is still endangered, the American alligator —with the help of farms like this one— has made an amazing comeback in just a few decades.

ALLIGATOR LAWS

States oversee alligator hunting to make sure the animals won't become endangered again. For example, all alligator hunters in Florida must have a state-issued permit. Even then, they can only use certain weapons. In Louisiana, it's illegal to ship alligator skins out of state without special tags.

Other laws control nonhunting interactions between people and alligators. In Florida and Texas, it's illegal to feed alligators. If caught doing so, the offender must pay a $500 fine. They might even go to jail for 60 days! These states don't want alligators looking for food to approach people.

illegal PETS

In some states, it's illegal for an alligator to be kept as a pet. Others require people to get a permit from the state government. In Connecticut, a person proven guilty of having a pet alligator faces up to 3 months in jail and a fine of up to $500.

Some states punish people who feed wild alligators. It's dangerous for both alligators and people.

NUISANCE ALLIGATORS

Alligators can become a problem when they live near people. If these alligators are more than 4 feet (1.2 m) long, **aggressive**, or just not scared of people, they're called nuisance alligators and must be removed.

The Florida Alligator Management Program captures alligators in backyards, swimming pools, and other areas occupied by people. Special alligator trappers catch the animals. The trappers relocate alligators that are smaller than 4 feet (1.2 m) long. Larger alligators are killed, and their skins and meat are sold. Part of the sum pays the trapper, and the remaining money goes to the state.

city GATORS?

Sometimes alligators are found in cities. These are often pets that are no longer wanted because they grew too large or became too hard to take care of. There are stories of alligators living in the New York City sewers, but cold winters and pollution make this unlikely.

Small alligators usually won't hunt anything bigger than a turtle. If they're aggressive, they're still considered dangerous.

ALLIGATOR DIET

An alligator's diet is another reason they don't make good pets. In the wild, they eat many different kinds of animals. Baby alligators eat insects, small fish, and frogs. As they grow, they hunt crabs, fish, and small birds. An adult alligator's meals include beavers, raccoons, snakes, turtles, and even deer. Alligators only have to eat once a week in the wild because they store fat in their tail.

An alligator's jaws are so powerful they can crush turtle shells. Its stomach is also strong. An alligator can **digest** anything it swallows, including feathers and bones!

alligator CANNIBALS

Alligator mothers can be aggressive in protecting their eggs and new hatchlings. They often charge at people who get close to a nest. While still small, baby alligators are prey for many animals, including other alligators. After a few years, young alligators don't have to worry about being eaten by anything—except bigger alligators!

Some turtles have shells that make them too hard to eat.

This turtle looks like it might escape!

Alligators hide in the water, blending in with plants and logs while waiting for a meal.

the death ROLL

If an alligator's prey is small enough, it's swallowed whole. However, if the prey is large, the alligator does a "death roll." The reptile grabs its prey and uses its powerful tail to spin over and over in the water. The animal drowns, and the alligator tears it into pieces.

Alligators hunt by surprise. An alligator stays motionless in the water until an animal comes near. Its tail then helps it **lunge** forward. It can push itself 5 feet (1.5 m) out of the water to snatch animals from trees! After the alligator grabs its prey, the reptile pulls it underwater to drown it.

Even though alligators can grow to be quite large, they can move fast. On land, they run at a top speed of 11 miles (18 km) per hour for a short distance. They swim much faster—about 20 miles (32 km) per hour.

ALLIGATOR ATTACKS

Alligators are more active on warmer days, especially during the summer months. People also spend more time outside, sometimes swimming to cool down. Therefore, the summer months are the most likely time for alligator attacks.

Kaleb Langdale was 17 years old when he was attacked by an 11-foot (3.4 m) alligator. He had been swimming in Florida's Caloosahatchee River when an alligator bit his arm. The alligator did a death roll, pulling off Langdale's arm but allowing him to swim away. Luckily, Langdale got to the hospital in time to save his life.

terrible BITE

When a cat or a dog bites, it might hurt a lot, but you don't have to worry about losing a body part. An alligator's bite is incredibly strong, even stronger than a lion's! Any animal that can pull or bite off an arm is definitely too dangerous to be around people.

Always pay attention to signs like these.

Remember, alligators are silent hunters.

Powerful, quick movements like this surprise an alligator's prey.

In Florida alone, alligators have killed 22 people since 1948. More than 300 people have reported injuries ranging from minor bites to loss of a limb. Although most survive attacks, the bite isn't the only danger. Many different types of germs can be found in the mouth of an alligator.

In July 2004, a woman was attacked from behind by an alligator near a pond. Though greatly injured, she survived for a time. However, pond and alligator **bacteria** gave her a deadly **infection**. One study found 38 kinds of bacteria in an alligator's mouth.

scary old GRANDPA

Alligators attack pets if they get a chance. A man had been walking his dog around a lake near St. Petersburg, Florida, when the dog was snatched by an 11-foot (3.4 m) alligator. The alligator was well known in the neighborhood and had even been named "Old Grandpa."

ALLIGATOR DEFENSE

An alligator's bite is more than a hundred times stronger than a person's bite. A person could never force an alligator's mouth open, but they can fight back in other ways. If an alligator catches someone, the victim should punch the reptile in the nose, eyes, or ears!

Sixteen-year-old Corey Workman of Florida was throwing rocks into a lake late at night. Suddenly, an alligator lunged out of the water. It grabbed his foot and dragged him into the lake. Corey remembered a lesson he saw on TV. He poked the alligator in the eye with his thumb as hard as he could. Luckily, the alligator let go.

small alligator BRAINS

Alligators seem sneaky, but they don't have big brains. An alligator's brain would only fill about half a tablespoon! These animals act mostly on **instinct**. If something moves, an alligator will try to eat it. A pet alligator might think this way about another pet—or even you!

The muscles that open an alligator's jaws are weak compared to the ones it uses to chomp down. That's why it's possible for this man to hold them shut.

ALLIGATORS' IMPORTANCE

You might wonder why we don't let alligators become extinct if they're so dangerous. They're very important to their **habitats**. Alligators keep animal populations under control. They also create tunnels and dens in the waterways. During the dry season, these "alligator holes" hold water. This helps not only alligators but also other animals—such as fish, frogs, turtles, and crabs—stay wet and cool.

Birds like to build their nests near alligator holes. During the dry season, the hole might be the only source of water for miles. Sometimes the animals living in or near the alligator hole become meals for the alligator that made the hole!

alligator NESTS

Before laying her eggs, a female alligator creates a nest from crushed plants. The nests are built on high ground so they won't flood. They're about 2 to 4 feet (0.6 to 1.2 m) tall and 7 feet (2.1 m) wide. The nests later become sources of food and shelter for other animals.

Mother alligators usually lay 35 to 50 eggs. If the temperature of the nest is above 93°F (34°C), the eggs hatch as males. If the nest is below 86°F (30°C), female alligators hatch!

INCREASING ATTACKS

Alligator attacks don't happen very often, but the number of attacks has increased over the years. Why? First, the alligator population has grown due to the strict protection laws. Second, the number of people living in the alligator's habitat has exploded. Homes, golf courses, and other buildings are often built near bodies of water where alligators live. The more people and alligators live near each other, the greater the chance of attacks.

If you're in alligator territory, always be aware of your surroundings and *never* approach any alligator, big or small.

armed with KNOWLEDGE

People often put themselves in danger because they don't know enough about alligators. That's why they feed alligators and approach alligator nests. They may swim in waters that are occupied by alligators, too. Now you know how dangerous all these behaviors are. Tell others and save lives!

Only special officials are allowed to handle alligators.
Never approach any alligator by yourself.

GLOSSARY

aggressive: ready to attack

bacteria: tiny creatures that can only be seen with a microscope

digest: to break down food inside the body so that the body can use it

dormant: in an inactive state, when bodily functions slow or stop

endangered: in danger of dying out

environment: the natural world in which a plant or animal lives

extinct: no longer living

gland: a body part that produces something needed for a bodily function

habitat: the natural place where an animal or plant lives

infection: the spread of germs inside the body, causing illness

instinct: an inborn reaction or behavior that aids in survival

lunge: a sudden forward motion

snout: an animal's nose and mouth

FOR MORE INFORMATION

Books

Potts, Steve. *American Alligators.* North Mankato, MN: Capstone Press, 2012.

Zobel, Derek. *Alligators.* Minneapolis, MN: Bellwether Media, 2012.

Websites

Fact Sheets: American Alligator
nationalzoo.si.edu/animals/reptilesamphibians/facts/factsheets/americanalligator.cfm
Learn more about the alligator life cycle from the National Zoo.

How Alligators Work
science.howstuffworks.com/environmental/life/zoology/reptiles-amphibians/alligator.htm
Read some cool facts about alligators.

Reptiles: Alligator & Crocodile
www.sandiegozoo.org/animalbytes/t-crocodile.html
The San Diego Zoo provides plenty of reptile facts and even sound clips.

INDEX